# Vaccinations

## Staying Healthy

# You can get sick.

Look at this.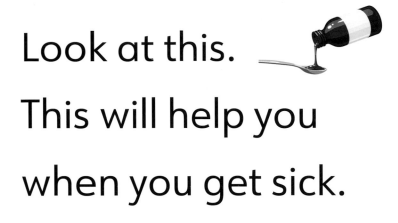
This will help you
when you get sick.

Look at this.
This will help you
when you get sick.

Look at this.

This will help you, too.

It will help you,

to stay healthy.

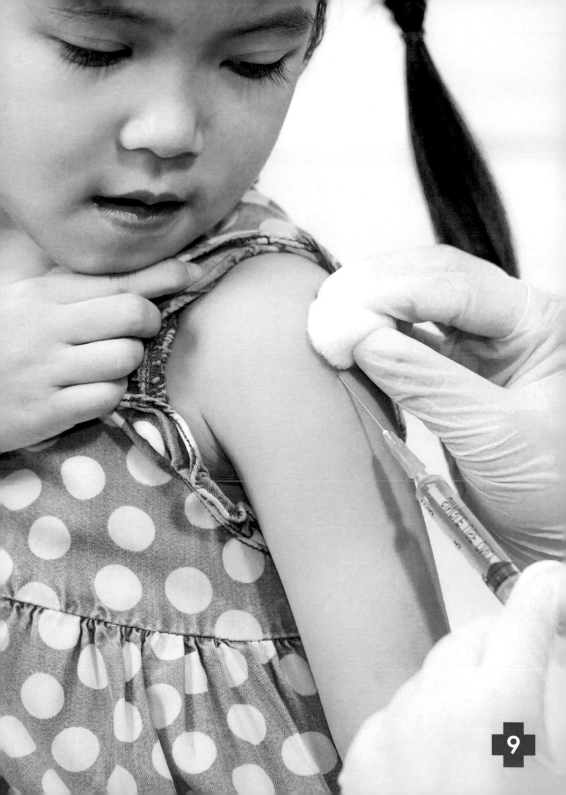

This is for my baby.

It will help my baby,

to stay healthy.

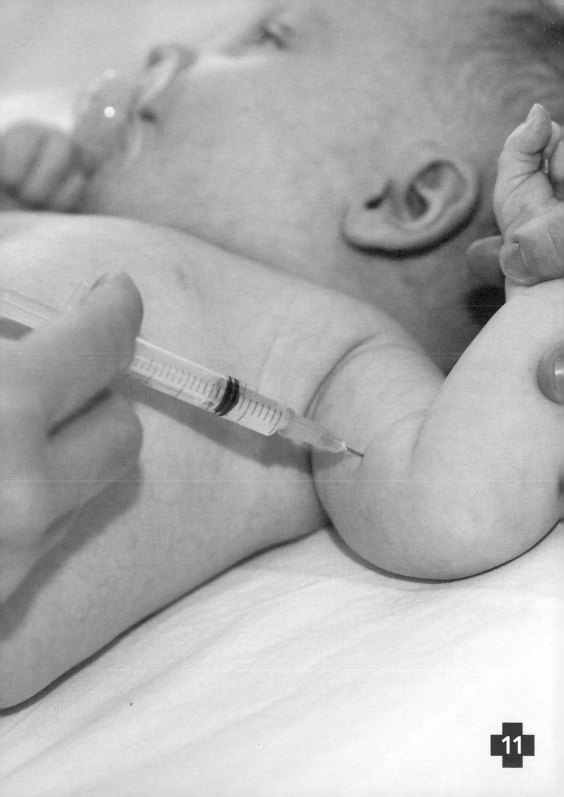

11

This is for

my big brother.

It will help my brother,

to stay healthy.

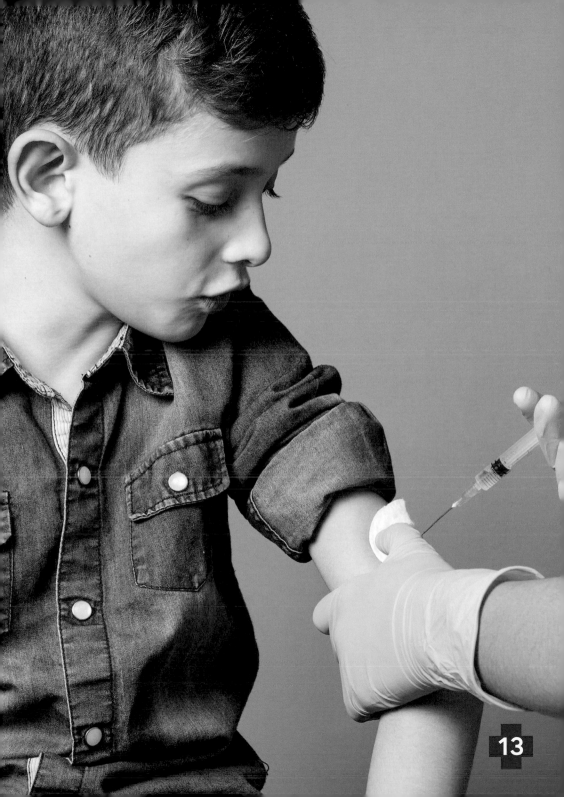

Look at the people.
The people will
stay healthy, too.

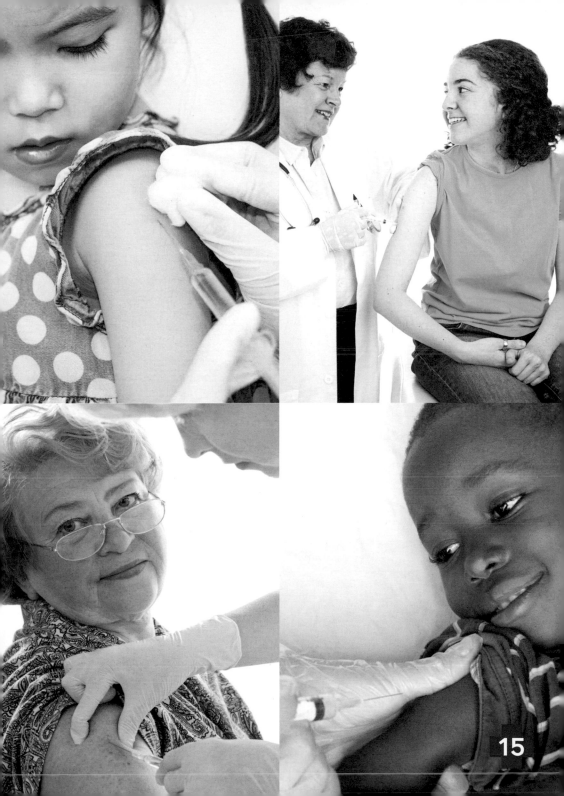

# We will all stay healthy.